D0569196

BORING
CAR TRIVIA
Volume 2

Written by Richard Porter

Second edition

Effort has been made to ensure the information in this book is accurate and honest but, as always, mistakes happen. If you're going to write in to complain, please remember to start your message with the words, "Oh dear, oh dear, oh dear. I simply cannot believe…"

ISBN: 9798572072303

sniffpetrol.com

CONTENTS

INTRODUCTION

In summer 2020 I compiled the first Sniff Petrol book of boring car trivia, ironically to stave off boredom, and was heartened/terrified to discover that many other people shared my enthusiasm for incredibly arcane facts. The first book went down so well I immediately set to work on a follow up, only to get distracted by other jobs (or, more likely, because I fell down an internet wormhole containing information about the Renault Sport Spider or the headlights on the E32 7 Series) and it took a bit longer than expected. Still, I got there in the end and this is the result. Unlike the last book, this one isn't divided into categories because I decided it would be more fun to make it a random grab bag of nerdish nonsense in which you never know what's coming next. Otherwise, it's business as usual. I hope you enjoy this book, and that it brings you a deep and restful night's sleep.

Richard Porter, Sniff Petrol
November 2020

FOREWORD
by Jeremy Clarkson

There is something quite peculiar about Richard Porter. What's worse, he seems determined to demonstrate this in print. I haven't read this second volume of his boring trivia series but I can tell you it will be deliberately dull and contain far too many things about the Rover 800. Don't say I didn't warn you.

Jeremy Clarkson

The heavy facelift of the Rover 800 in 1991 was compromised because the designers were told they must carry over the doors from the previous model, only to discover too late in the development process that the panel presses for the old doors were worn out and had to be replaced anyway.

If it wasn't for Bernie Ecclestone, the Ford RS200 would have been designed by Gordon Murray. Ford wanted Murray to create their Group B car, and Murray was keen, but he worked for Brabham at the time and team boss Ecclestone wasn't happy with his star designer taking on other work.

*

Although the Renault Sport Spider of 1995 was famously launched with no windscreen, all 96 right-hand-drive cars officially imported into the UK came with the optional 'screen fitted.

*

The Vauxhall/Opel Zafira was sold in Japan as the Subaru Traviq. Weirdly, GM Japan also sold the Zafira as an Opel but its cars came from Germany while the Subaru-branded ones were built in Thailand which made them cheaper to buy.

*

The last ever Morris-badged vehicle was the van version of the Austin Metro. It was built until 1985 when the Morris name was retired and the Metro van re-badged as an Austin.

*

When Porsche entered its 959 rally cars in the 1985 Rallye des Pharaons in Egypt to try them out ahead of the Paris-Dakar, the support vehicle was a Mercedes G-wagen which Porsche's motorsport department had fitted with the V8 from a 928.

*

The only exterior panels in common between the standard Austin Metro and the MG Metro 6R4 were the doors. And even then, the rally car ones had extra pods at their rear edges.

The Toyota GR Yaris homologation special shares only seven exterior parts with the regular Yaris hatchback; headlights (x2), tail lights (x2), door mirrors (x2), and the roof antenna.

*

When Fiat marketing boss Luigi Maglione was invited to view a prototype of the original Panda he observed that the inside of the car was incomplete with several major parts obviously missing and was surprised to be told that no, this was the finished interior.

*

In order to persuade Britain's most powerful company car buyers that the newly-announced Rover 800 was the car for them, Austin Rover chartered an Aer Lingus 747 and flew a bunch of fleet managers to Switzerland to try out the 800 range and hear ARG boss Harold Musgrove telling them how brilliant it was. The event was a great success until the chartered jet arrived back at Birmingham Airport and accidentally taxied into the terminal building.

*

BMW took the unusual step of revealing the Z1 roadster before it had decided to put it into production because a German journalist visiting one of their facilities accidentally saw one of two experimental prototypes built to assess the car's unusual construction. It was two more years before the Z1 went on sale.

*

The Citroën AX came with a space in each door trim designed to accommodate a one litre bottle.

*

The BLS is the only Cadillac never to be sold in the US. It was based on the SAAB 9-3 and built alongside it in Trollhättan, Sweden, for customers in Europe and other non-North American markets. No one was much interested, sales were low and it was deleted after just three years.

*

The new Defender is the first Land Rover since the original Discovery of 1989 (and its Discovery II relative) not to feature a clamshell bonnet.

*

When designing the XJ40 one of Jaguar's priorities was to make it less complicated to build than the car it would replace. Hence the new car's bonnet was made of just two pieces, where the old cars was knitted together from 27 separate parts.

*

The 1992 MG RV8 used headlights from the contemporary Porsche 911. The German company was happy for MG to borrow these parts on the understanding that the forward upper edge of the light unit was not exposed, as it was on a 911, as it considered this to be a signature design feature.

*

The Peugeot 205 T16 Group B rally car used the gearbox from the Citroën SM.

*

To get people interested in the new Renault 4 of 1961, 200 examples were dumped on the streets of Paris and passing punters were invited to get in and go for a spin in a promotional event called 'Take the Wheel'. There was a Renault employee in the passenger seat of each car to make sure no thievery occurred.

*

Names considered for the original Ford Mustang included Torino, Cougar, Avventura [sic], and Allegro.

In the early eighties BL proudly boasted that its Longbridge factory used as much electricity as the whole of Oxford.

*

The DeLorean DMC-12 might have died in 1982 but, thanks to a 1989 contract with Universal signed around the time of Back To The Future Part II, John Z. DeLorean continued to make money out of it, receiving five percent of net receipts on all BTTF merchandising and commercial tie-ups that featured the DMC-12.

*

The Fiat 500 of 1957 came with a retractable canvas sunroof as standard, not out of generosity on Fiat's part but because canvas was cheaper than metal and cutting a big hole in the roof saved the company a fortune in steel.

*

The TV advert for the launch of the 1990 Rover Metro was directed by Ridley Scott.

*

After the fall of the Berlin Wall in 1989 West Germany suffered a used VW Golf drought as eager East Germans, realising there was more to cars than Wartburgs and Trabants, raced to snap up second-hand Western models, the Golf being the most popular.

*

At the start of the nineties Morgan switched from Smiths to VDO gauges to the horror of some trad Morgan customers, especially in Germany, who asked if the dials could still have 'Smiths' written on them. VDO, perhaps understandably, said no.

*

Tiff Needell's actual first name is Timothy.

Tifosi, the name given to Ferrari F1 fans, literally means 'infected with typhoid'. It's meant to suggest people who are acting crazy due to fever.

*

The 2007 Subaru Impreza WRX STI Spec C Type RA-R was a lightened, lowered, extra hardcore Japan-only model of which just 300 were made. Its full name without any of the abbreviations would be the Subaru Impreza World Rally eXperimental, Subaru Technica International, Specification Competition, Type Record Attempt - Radical.

*

In 1996 Rover replaced the Honda V6 in its 800 Series with the brand new, home grown KV6 engine. To mark this, Car magazine conducted a group test with the new model in its April '96 issue, the opening spread of which featured the participants photographed inside Wembley Stadium under the headline 'THEY THINK IT'S ALL ROVER… IT IS NOW'.

*

When Lotus first pitched to do something exciting with a Vauxhall/Opel saloon their proposal was based on the Senator. GM asked the Norfolkian engineers to look instead at the next model down in the range and the Lotus Carlton/Omega was the result.

*

The Jaguar X-type's headlights were inspired by the shape of the engine intakes on the de Havilland Comet airliner. An abandoned X-type facelift would have evolved the shape to mirror the intakes on the Comet-based Hawker Siddeley Nimrod.

*

One of Nigel Mansell's middle names is Ernest.

15

From 1962 onwards the screen washer on the VW Beetle was powered using air pressure from the spare tyre. The spare was deliberately over-inflated to provide plenty of oomph, and a valve shut when the tyre was down to the correct pressure for use on the car so you could never strand yourself if you got a puncture just after an enthusiastic bout of screen washing.

Ayrton Senna has a road named after him in Reading. The Brazilian driver lived in the suburb of Tilehurst for a couple of years in his early career, moving out of his rented house around 1984. In 1995, the year after he died, Reading council named a new street in his honour. Disappointingly, it is a dead end and has speed bumps along it. Tilehurst is also home to the Ayrton Senna children's play area.

The grille badge on the Bugatti Chiron is made of sterling silver and weighs 150 grams. Bugatti engineers said it was the only part of the car that was "allowed to be heavy". Although, at 630 kilos, the car's entire powertrain weighs more than an Ariel Atom.

*

The first Mercedes CLS came about because designer Michael Fink was a big fan of Jaguars and idly wondered what a 'Jaguar by Mercedes' would look like. Management got wind of his sketches, liked what they saw, and made the car an official project.

*

The minimalist interpretation of the Rover badge seen on the front of early SD1s was created by Ian Beech, a member of the Rover studio team who had trained in jewellery design. He went on to style the rather less jewellery-like Austin Maestro.

*

Tony Mason is best known as a rally co-driver turned snowball-to-the-face BBC rally coverage presenter and Top Gear steam rally doyenne. But between these two careers he set up a successful car accessories business which expanded to sell rally-orientated clothes including scarves, bobble hats and jackets.

*

During development of the joint Rover-Honda project that became the 800 and Legend, Japanese engineers switched their new V6 engine from three to four valves per cylinder. This made the engine taller and wider, necessitating an increase in the track width of the cars that would use it. The styling for both was close to sign off but Rover hastily reworked their car to smoothly integrate wider wings while Honda accommodated the change more crudely, which is why the first-generation Honda Legend has Audi Quattro-style box arches.

*

In Japan the second-generation Subaru Legacy Outback was called the Legacy Lancaster.

*

The man who oversaw the Land Rover Discovery 3, chief designer Andy Wheel, never much liked the body colour wheelarches of the updated Discovery 4 to the extent that he ordered a set of the original black plastic arches and had them fitted to his Discovery 4 company car.

*

If you like driving your Bugatti Chiron with fresh air in your face, don't go over 92mph. At that speed the car automatically closes its windows as it makes itself as aerodynamic as possible for high-speed stability.

*

Nissan writes the name of its first electric car as LEAF because it's an acronym for "Leading Environmentally friendly Affordable Family car".

*

Prototypes of the Rover P6 were painted an unremarkable generic grey, intended to make the secret cars blend in during on-road testing. However, it was decided that this grey rather suited the P6's shape and was adopted for production, labelled in brochures as 'City Grey'.

*

The Renault Clio was sold in Japan as the Renault Lutécia as Honda had a domestic dealer chain called Clio. Lutécia is derived from Lutetia, the ancient Roman city that became the Paris of today. The separate Honda Clio dealer network, which sold 'traditional' Hondas like the Accord, was abandoned in 2006.

Possible names for the Morris Marina included Morris Monaco, Morris Mamba, Morris Maori, Morris Musketeer, and Morris Machete. The final shortlist was Morris Major, Morris Mirage, Morris Mistral and Morris Marina. The latter was chosen for production, although it was already what they called the Morris 1100/1300 in Denmark. The Danish importer solved the problem of a confusing name clash by discontinuing the old 1100 shape car when imports of the new Marina started in 1972.

*

The styling of the 1991 TVR Griffith was the baby of the company's chief engineer, John Ravenscroft. When company boss Peter Wheeler oversaw the design for the subsequent, and less classically pretty, Chimaera sister car it was Ravenscroft who came up with the unofficial internal codename UP1 which stood, rather uncharitably, for 'Ugly Pig One'.

*

The Reliant Scimitar SS1 used Triumph TR7 seat frames.

*

In 1986 Honda UK pulled advertising from Car magazine after a critical review of the then-new Integra, huffily accusing the report of being 'subjective' and 'vindictive' and writer Richard Bremner of having 'scant understanding' of Honda.

*

Integrale might signal a tasty version of the Lancia Delta but in Italy it's also the word that denotes the wholemeal type of pasta.

*

Volkswagen Group overlord Ferdinand Piëch hated hotel room air conditioning so much he would travel the world with a small tool kit which would enable him to remove normally sealed windows to get a flow of fresh air.

*

The original Porsche 924 got stick for having a 'van engine' (the EA831 from the Audi 100 but also used in the VW LT van) yet was rarely criticised for its rear suspension which was from the VW 1302 'Super Beetle'. Its front suspension used many parts from the mk1 Golf.

*

The MG Metro 6R4 rally car was assembled at Austin Rover's Longbridge plant in a building called Dalmuir because its structure originally stood in Dalmuir near Glasgow where, between 1915 and 1929, it was used to make submarines. It was bought by Austin in the late 1930s, dismantled and re-erected in Birmingham.

*

The 1997-2010 WRC rules stipulated that cars had to be a minimum of 4000mm long, a problem for Peugeot which wanted to enter the 3835mm-long 206. To get around the problem they built 4000 Grand Tourisme special editions fitted with strangely distended bumpers which took the car's length up to the mandated minimum.

*

During development of the Volkswagen L1 concept, which became the limited production XL1, VW engineers borrowed a Light Car Company Rocket to benchmark.

*

The Iveco Daily van much beloved of Tesco home delivery fleets uses the same automatic gearbox as the Rolls-Royce Phantom. It's the 8HP70, made by ZF.

*

In Japan the 1995 Fiat Bravo was called the Fiat Bravissimo.

During development of its brand-new hybrid-powered black cab, LEVC wanted to test the car in its natural habitat without attracting too much attention so it took prototypes into central London in the dead of night only to find that people on the streets still recognised the test cars as taxis, even in complete camo wrap, and kept trying to flag them down.

*

The only V12-powered Japanese production car in history is the second-generation Toyota Century, built from 1997 until 2017.

*

One of the lead designers on MG's ZR, ZS and ZT was Harris Mann, the chap who designed the Austin Allegro, Triumph TR7 and Austin Princess.

*

In the 2000s Honda started developing a large, V8-powered, rear-wheel-drive executive car to take on Lexus, BMW and Mercedes. The project was cancelled in late 2008 after global economies tanked and Honda profits took a dive. The same round of cutbacks also culled the never-seen front-engined, V10-powered, all-wheel-drive NSX mk2.

*

The Vauxhall/Opel Signum was developed because the company was due to kill off the Omega without replacement and Opel executives wanted something else in which to be chauffeur driven. Hence the Signum majored on rear seat space and comfort.

*

The first-generation Aston Martin Vanquish was too small of a project to go through the labyrinthine programme approval process of behemoth Ford which owned Aston at the time. Instead, then-Aston boss Bob Dover got Ford overlord Jac Nasser to sign off the car in a hotel bar one evening during the 1998 Geneva motor show where the Project Vantage concept was on display. Nasser gave the go-ahead with the words, "You will do this, and I will get my money back".

*

The 2017-onwards Audi A8 can detect an imminent side impact and use its air suspension to raise the car on the side about to be hit, thereby directing impact forces into the sills and floor of the shell which are stronger than the doors. Audi claims the system can jack up the exposed side of the car by up to 80mm within half a second, reducing the load on the car's occupants by up to 50 percent. The same trick can be performed by the 2020 Mercedes S-Class.

*

The Alfa Romeo Junior Z had a shorter rear overhang than the Alfa Spider on which it was based, leaving no room for the fuel tank. The solution was to borrow the smaller tank from the Montreal until the 1600 Junior Z came along in 1973 at which point the rear overhang grew 10cm in order to use the standard Spider floorpan and tank, to the chagrin of Junior Z designer Ercole Spada.

*

The original Rover SD1, launched in 1976, had a symmetrical dashboard, theoretically making it cheaper and easier to build left- and right-hand-drive versions. The instruments were in a separate box that sat on top of the main dash moulding on the driver's side and the redundant hole for the steering column on the passenger's side was filled with an air vent.

The VE-shape Holden Commodore of 2006 came with a SAAB-style 'night panel' feature that turned off the illumination of all non-essential gauges. Unlike SAABs, which operated the feature with a dedicated button, the Holden activated this mode if the driver simultaneously held down the plus and minus buttons for the instrument illumination adjuster.

*

The pumps within the engine cooling system of the Bugatti Chiron could brim a bath in 12 seconds.

*

In the later days of MG Rover the large car assembly line at Longbridge was a powerful testament to the factory's car production skills, building a complex matrix of different models on one line. There were Rover 75s and MG ZTs, saloons and estates, and front- and rear-wheel-drive drivetrains, all in various combinations and all coming down the same track, plus special order 'Monogram' paint finishes which were completely line-built where other factories would spray low run colours off-line. Getting this broad assortment of possible combinations built on the same line was such a feat that engineers from other car companies used to visit Longbridge to see how it was done.

*

The radio aerial on the Skoda Favorit GLXie was built into the sunroof.

*

When Ford engineers wanted to give the Escort replacement an independent rear axle they had to prove they could do it within strict cost targets. Initially this seemed a tall order until they realised they could adapt the independent rear end from the Mondeo estate and get costs down by using cheaply pressed parts rather than fancy and expensive cast items. Before the independent axle was signed off, work continued in parallel to make a twist beam rear end, just in case the more sophisticated solution was nixed by accountants. This work wasn't wasted, as the experience gained was used to improve the chassis of the last generation Escort.

*

Shortly after the Morris Marina was launched in 1971, Leyland engineers became concerned that the offside side windscreen wiper would lift from its resting place at speed, impairing the driver's view. One solution to this problem would have been to fit a heavier wiper arm but BL rejected this on cost grounds and went for the simpler solution of flipping the wipers on RHD cars to the LHD configuration and vice versa, thereby saddling the Marina with 'wrong way round' wipers that left an unwiped bit of screen in the top corner of the driver's side.

*

Early examples of the 1947 Renault 4CV were painted sand yellow because the company was using up paint left behind by occupying German forces that had commandeered its factory during the Second World War to build armoured vehicles for use in the deserts of Libya and Egypt. The distinctive colour earned the car the nickname 'La motte de beurre' or 'the ball of butter'.

*

In order to withstand the rigours of city driving, the GPO used to order vans from Morris, including Series Zs, J-types and Minors, with the metal wings replaced by facsimiles made from unpainted black rubber.

The first new car of the 21st century was the Rover 45 which was officially revealed on 4 January 2000.

*

The 2000-off Mini Cooper S Works GP of 2006 – officially called the Mini Cooper S with John Cooper Works GP kit – was assembled by Bertone in Italy. It was the only first generation Mini with a third brake light at the bottom of the rear screen glass because its bespoke tailgate spoiler blocked the normal third brake light at the top of the tailgate, the hole for which was plugged by a plastic fillet. Mounting the central brake light at the base of the rear glass was made possible because the rear wiper, which would normally sit there, was deleted, supposedly to save weight.

*

In 2013 Mercedes-Benz became the first car maker to attach QR codes to its cars giving emergency services access to information about the specific model and how safely to dismember it, avoiding airbag modules, high voltage cables et al, in the event of an accident. The code stickers are located inside the fuel filler and on the B-pillar in new models and available to be retro-fitted to Merc models from 1990 onwards.

*

Works-spec 'International' versions of the MG Metro 6R4 were built in right-hand-drive but had a left-hand-drive Metro dashboard, putting the instrument pack (and the vent controls) in front of the co-driver, leaving the driver with just a large rev counter to look at.

*

The seven-speed double-clutch gearbox in the Bugatti Veyron was developed by Ricardo in the UK using an old Lamborghini Diablo as a mule.

The only front-engined, rear-drive vehicle in VW's history is the LT van (the Taro pick-up, a re-badged Toyota Hilux, and the Argentinian Volkswagen 1500, a re-badged Chrysler Avenger, weren't really Volkswagens).

*

From 1950 until 1971 Austin made its J40 kids' pedal car in a factory in Bargoed, South Wales set up to provide employment for ex-miners with lung disease. The cars were made from metal offcuts sent over from the Austin factory in Longbridge, Birmingham. When pedal car production ended, the Bargoed works continued to produce metal parts for full-size British Leyland cars. The last part it made was the rocker cover for the A-series engine before the factory closed in 1999.

*

Since 1964 Playboy magazine has given its Playmate of the Year a free car. The first car to be given away was a Ford Mustang which, like all PotY freebie cars until 1975, was sprayed pink. Over the years, Playmates have received various Porsches, Jaguars and Corvettes, so spare a though for 2009 Playmate of the Year, Ida Ljungqvist, whose free car was a Mazda6.

*

In the late 1950s Rover planned to launch a tall, three-door estate based on the P4 saloon chassis, to be called the Road Rover. Ahead of the proto-crossover's announcement they contacted Corgi and allowed it, under a veil of great secrecy, to create a toy version which would be launched at the same time as the real thing. Rover then realised the Road Rover was too strange and unattractive to have any chance of success and scrapped it, leaving Corgi with all the tooling and box printing plates for a toy car they could never sell.

CARS THAT LOOKED LIKE THEY SHOULD BE HATCHBACKS (BUT WEREN'T)

Alfa Romeo Alfasud (pre-1980)
Audi Coupé
Austin Allegro
Austin Princess
Citroën C6
Citroën CX
Citroën GS
Ford Capri mk1
Lancia Gamma Berlina
Peugeot 104 (pre-facelift)

FERRARI ROAD CAR NUMBER NAMING
LOGIC SINCE 1975

288 – 2.8-litre*, eight cylinders
308 – 3.0-litre**, eight cylinders
328 – 3.2-litre, eight cylinders
348 – 3.4-litre, eight cylinders
F355 – 3.5-litre, five valves per cylinder
360 – 3.6-litre engine, plus a zero on the end
400 – Capacity per cylinder, rounded down from 401.9cc
412 – Capacity per cylinder, rounded up from 411.8cc
F430 – 4.3-litre engine, plus a zero on the end
456 – 456cc per cylinder
458 – 4.5-litre, eight cylinder
488 – 488cc per cylinder
512 – 5-litre***, 12 cylinder
512 TR/F512 M – 5-litre***, 12 cylinder
550 – 5.5-litre, plus a zero on the end
575 – Engine capacity (5748cc) rounded up
599 – Engine capacity (5999cc) minus last number
612 – 6-litre****, 12 cylinder
812 – Eight (hundred) horsepower, 12 cylinders

* Actually 2855cc
** Actually 2927cc
*** Actually 4943cc
**** Actually 5748cc

The E32-shape BMW 7 Series was the first car in the world to be available with xenon headlights.

*

The W140-shape Mercedes S-class, considered to be the last of the over-engineered Benzes, took ten years to develop and went so over-budget that following its (behind schedule) debut the project's chief engineer, Dr Wolfgang Peter, suffered the ignominy of being 'moved sideways' into Mercedes' truck division.

*

The very first Lada officially came off the production line on what would have been Lenin's 100th birthday, 22 April 1970. This was almost certainly deliberate timing, not that it mattered to Lenin who had been dead for 46 years.

*

To aid reversing, the slanted upper bootlid of the Lancia Gamma Berlina had an extra window sunk into it, hidden behind a louvred cover. When Motor Sport magazine road tested the Gamma in 1978 they described this feature as 'strange'.

*

In the early 2000s a Mercedes-Benz engineer spent a year scouring the world for the best button action. The conclusion of his research was that the ideal button 'throw' was 1.4mm and future Mercedes switches were designed accordingly. All Benz button suppliers were issued with a finger pressure graph and soft-feel paint spec so that every single button felt the same no matter where it came from.

*

The first automotive application of hot formed steel was in the side impact beams of the SAAB 9000.

Land Rover began developing a shortened version of the Discovery 3's 'T5' platform for a smaller 'Discovery Sport' before deciding instead to use the short-wheelbase chassis for a more upmarket car which became the 2005 Range Rover Sport. This was a wise move since the first generation Sport turned out to be the company's most profitable model.

*

Chevrolet UK celebrated Jason Plato's 2010 BTCC drivers' championship win in a Chevrolet Cruze by offering a CS (Chevrolet Sport) pack as an option on road-going Cruze models. The £1595 pack consisted of a bodykit and suspension tuned by the RML race team. Embarrassingly, the pack also included white-painted wheels made by Rimstock, the family firm of Plato's hated rival, Matt Neal.

*

The first-generation Smart ForFour didn't have a parcel shelf.

*

Ferdinand Piëch insisted that Volkswagens came with flock linings for gloveboxes, door bins and other storage compartments as a simple piece of buyer psychology, arguing that it was worth the expense because potential customers would think, wow, if they've done that in there, imagine how good the inside of the engine must be.

*

The high level of interior detailing in the Volkswagen Golf mk4 extended to the parcel shelf which featured retractor mechanisms on the strings that made it rise with the tailgate so that if these were unhooked they disappeared neatly into the shelf itself rather than dangling messily.

When Land Rover started project Remus to put a new dashboard in the original Range Rover they commissioned a supplier to give the car one-touch electric windows for the first time. The supplier got the system working on their test rigs and sent samples over to the factory only to receive a call from Land Rover saying the anti-trap rollback feature didn't work, allowing the window to get almost to the top of its travel before tripping the safety system and retracting the glass again. The supplier was puzzled, insisting that they were working to an industry standard tolerance of just a few millimetres. Well there's your problem then, replied Land Rover engineers, the old Range Rover doors are built to a tolerance about three times that.

*

The 1985 Subaru XT drove its front wheels in normal running but switched to four-wheel-drive if the wipers were turned on. It would also punt drive to the rear under braking or when kickdown was activated since, strangely, this system was only applied to the automatic model.

*

During early development of the MG F engineers wanted to test and calibrate the K-series engine for a mid-engined installation so they bought four second-hand mk1 Toyota MR2s on which they could perform heart transplants. To avoid giving away what they were up to, each of these Toyotas was bought from a Midlands MR2 specialist over the course of six months and paid for with a personal cheque by a Rover employee posing as a regular punter.

*

Any Fiat Barchetta built between 1995 and 2002 contained a hand-written travellers' prayer on a tiny piece of paper hidden somewhere in the car. This was a practise among the workers at the Maggiora plant in Chivasso where the cars were assembled. When Maggiora went bust in 2002 Barchetta production was moved in-house to Fiat's Mirafiori plant and the prayers ceased to be standard equipment.

*

The Camargue of 1975 was the first Rolls-Royce to be designed using metric measurements.

*

By the 1990s most new cars used air-blending heaters. Two exceptions were the MG F and Ford Fiesta which featured old fashioned water valve heaters. In the MG's case it was because there was no room for an air-blending system. Ford opted for a more compact water-valve set-up because it helped with crash performance, though they also sold it as quicker to warm up on the kind of short urban journeys for which many Fiestas were used. Later on, another car to use an anomalous water valve heater was the V8-engined version of the MG ZT and Rover 75, again for packaging reasons.

*

In the 1950s Mercedes-Benz engineers would test the durability of prototypes over a few kilometres of unmade forest track near their Stuttgart base. During the sixties they discovered that the track was due to be paved so, before the re-surfacing machines arrived, they took plaster casts of its surface and used these to have the track replicated in concrete at their R&D centre. The track surface was subsequently digitised and is still used to this day during 'torture' cycles on suspension test rigs.

*

The Ford Sierra and the Ferrari F40 had the same drag coefficient; 0.34.

The first-generation Rover 200, launched in 1984, used the suspension settings from the Honda Ballade upon which it was based since its Japanese designers insisted that no changes were necessary. After early complaints about the car's poor handling Rover decided to investigate and discovered that the spring rates on the rear axle differed by up to 17 percent side-to-side. The British engineers fixed the problem and their changes were so effective that they were later adopted by Honda too.

*

Tony Crook used to claim that only one person had ever died at the wheel of a Bristol, and that was from a self-inflicted shotgun wound.

*

The 1995 Vauxhall/Opel Vectra featured a small plastic tool clipped inside the fuel filler that allowed you to remove the tyre valve caps without getting your hands dirty. The feature was later extended to other GM cars.

*

When Lamborghini announced the 20-off Reventón at the 2007 Frankfurt show, it intended each car to end up with a loyal and trusted customer. So imagine their delight when, in 2009, it became known that one example had somehow ended up in the hands of unlovely Chechen president (and former warlord) Ramzan Kadyrov.

*

In the early sixties a planned increase in production at Austin's Longbridge factory presented the problem of where to store all the completed cars before they were dispatched to dealers. The answer was to build a nine-floor, 3300 space storage facility next to the assembly halls which was, upon completion in 1961, the largest multi-storey car park in the world.

For the 1997 Frankfurt Show BMW decided to give a sneak preview of the 21st century Mini, partly to show the world a new Mini was on its way and partly to suck the wind from the reveal of the Mercedes A-Class which was happening at the same event. To tantalise the press, the new car would be driven across the stage during an eve-of-the-show BMW event but there was a problem; the design had only just been signed off and there were no running prototypes to production spec. The solution was to cut-down a Fiat Punto and cover it with fibreglass moulds taken from the signed-off Mini clay buck to create a running design model convincing enough for its brief moment in the spotlight, complete with heavily tinted windows to stop anyone spotting the Fiat dashboard inside. It would be another three years before the production Mini arrived.

*

The roof of the 991-shape Porsche 911 GT3 RS was made of magnesium, saving 1.1kg and 800g over equivalent roofs made in aluminium and carbon fibre respectively. At the time there was only once place in the world capable of cutting magnesium to the right shape and only one place able to shape it correctly. Unluckily for Porsche's accountants, the former was in South Korea and the latter in Canada which is why each GT3 RS roof had a small world tour before fetching up in Stuttgart to be attached to the rest of the car.

*

The Austin Maxi almost came as a saloon as well as a hatchback. The four-door variant had made the running prototype stage before being cancelled and had to be clumsily edited out of the footage of pre-production testing that was shown at the car's launch.

The 6.2-litre, 797 horsepower Dodge Challenger SRT Hellcat Redeye has an eco mode.

In the mid-sixties, as part of their search for a western design to adapt as the Soviet Union's new people's car, the Central Scientific Research Automobile and Automotive Engines Institute in Moscow assessed a range of cars including the Renault 16, Ford Taunus 12M, Morris 1100, Peugeot 204 as well as the Škoda 1000 MB and Moskvitch-408 before declaring the Fiat 124 the best for conditions in the USSR. However, since the Renault 16 and Peugeot 204 only launched in March and April of 1965 respectively, and the Soviets signed a preliminary deal with Fiat on 1 July 1965, it seems likely the 124 was destined to win the comparison because it came from a country with a government sympathetic to Communism. When the deal was done eight Fiat 124s were shipped to Russia for testing and promptly began to disintegrate on the punishing local roads. This led to over 800 design changes before the car, known locally as the VAZ-2101 and in export markets as the Lada, went on sale in 1970. It was assembled in a brand-new factory built in Stavropol-on-Volga which was re-developed as a 'new city' for car production and re-named Tolyatti in honour of Palmiro Togliatti, leader of the Italian Communist Party from 1927 until his death in 1964, shortly after he had begun to grease the wheels that lead to Fiat's deal with the Soviets.

PLACES WHERE
THE FORD CAPRI WAS MADE
Cologne, Germany
Genk, Belgium
Halewood, UK
Port Elizabeth, South Africa
Sydney, Australia

*

In the mid-seventies GM decided the first-generation Holden Commodore should be based on the Opel Rekord/Senator and shipped a German-made prototype to Australia for local testing. It managed to cover just 1500 kilometres around the harsh, Aussie-spec roads of Holden's Lang Lang proving ground before it was written off. Another prototype was taken into the Outback for real-world testing and promptly split apart at the firewall. Opel engineers demanded to see the data from these tests and, upon receiving load gauge readings 300 percent higher than anything they'd observed in Europe, assumed Holden's engineers were using the equipment incorrectly. An Opel team was dispatched to Australia to see what was what and, having seen local conditions for themselves, worked with the Holden team to give the Commodore a re-designed shell with extra reinforcements, though not before one of the Germans had allegedly said that what Australia really needed was re-designed roads.

*

In its day the 1993 Nissan Serena 2-litre diesel, with its mighty 66bhp engine, could claim to be Britain's slowest new car boasting a 0-62 time of 31 seconds.

*

The Rover SD1 Vitesse was to be called Rapide but Aston Martin owned this name and wouldn't let Rover use it.

Two front-wheel-drive cars have worn the Maserati badge. The first was the ill-fated Quattroporte 2 of 1974 which was basically a stretched Citroën SM in a four-door Bertone body and, as a result of money troubles and cooling Maser-Citroënian relations, never homologated for sale in Europe. Only 12 were built. The second FWD car with a Maserati badge was the 1988 Chrysler TC, officially 'the Chrysler TC by Maserati', which was a re-bodied K-car fitted with turbocharged four-cylinder engines or a Mitsubishi V6 and assembled in Italy. It lasted just three years.

*

Subaru used to import right-hand-drive Legacy estates into the United States exclusively for the US Postal Service so that post delivery people could hop out kerbside to drop letters and parcels into mailboxes.

*

In the early 2000s Jaguar XJ220 owners starting using their cars sparingly, if at all, because it was impossible to get the bespoke Bridgestone tyres for them. That is until 2017 when not one but two tyre makers, Bridgestone and Pirelli, announced production of new, modern tyres in the XJ220's required size.

*

Renault CEO Georges Besse is the only car company boss to have vacated his position on account of being assassinated. On the evening of 17 November 1986 Besse was shot dead as he walked from his chauffeur-driven car to the door of his Paris home. Anti-capitalist group Action Directe claimed responsibility for the killing, saying it was in response to mass redundancies at Renault that resulted from Besse's plan to stem the company's financial losses.

CARS BASED ON THE GENERAL MOTORS J-CAR PLATFORM

Buick Skyhawk
Cadillac Cimarron
Chevrolet Cavalier
Chevrolet Chevair
Chevrolet Monza
Daewoo Espero/Aranos
Holden Camira
Isuzu Aska
Oldsmobile Firenza
Opel Ascona C
Pontiac Sunbird/J2000
Pontiac Sunfire
Toyota Cavalier*
Vauxhall Cavalier mk2

* A re-badged Chevy Cavalier only sold in Japan.

Although the UK is only a short ship ride from France, all three major French car makers have built cars in Britain at some point. Citroën assembled a whole range of cars at its Slough factory between 1926 and 1965, including the Traction Avant, 2CV, Ami 6, ID/DS and a funny little 2CV-based, UK-only coupé called the Bijou. Between 1949 and 1962 Renault built 4CVs and Dauphines in Acton (and between 2001 and 2014 Renault Trafic vans were assembled alongside their Vauxhall Vivaro sisters at GM's Luton plant). Finally, between 1985 and 2004 Peugeot built the 309, 405, 306 and 206 at the factory in Ryton, Coventry it had inherited after it bought Chrysler's European operations in the late seventies.

*

The smooth, disc-like wheels on the Jaguar XJ220 concept car were actually wheel trims attached over generic cross-spoke alloys.

*

The village of Wollaston in Northamptonshire might not seem like an automotive mecca but appearances can be deceiving. It's the location of the Scott Bader chemical factory that supplied TVR with the resins to make its fibreglass panels, it was the base for Auto Racing Technology, the company that, among other things, built the first six prototypes of the Ford RS200, and it was the original, long-time home of evo magazine. It also has quite a good fish & chip shop.

*

Since its foundation in 1968, Hot Wheels has made over six billion cars, more than the US Big Three combined have managed in their entire lifetimes. Hot Wheels currently produces over 10 million cars a week.

In the mid-seventies Vauxhall considered importing a right-hand-drive, Europeanised version of the 'downsized' Cadillac Seville, launched in 1975, to sit at the top of its range. The plan was abandoned because the car, though small for an American luxury car, was reckoned to be too large, too chintzy and too thirsty to work in Britain. Instead, Vauxhall got their flagships by adapting Opels to make the Carlton and Royale of 1978.

*

The first Porsche 924 test mule was a BMW 2002 with subtly swollen wheel arches.

*

During development of the mk3 Fiesta, launched in 1989, Ford engineers were so keen to unlock the handling secrets of the Peugeot 205 that they filmed super slow-motion video of 205s under hard cornering to understand how their suspension behaved. In the end they concluded that there were no particular secrets, and in fact discovered some undesirable behaviour such as a steering rack that moved around more than was ideal, and that the Peugeot's highly-rated handling had been set up less by science and more by the seat-of-the-pants.

*

When Proton was able to offer a three-valves-per-cylinder version of the eight valve, four-cylinder Mitsubishi engine it had been using in its early cars it labelled the new motor 'Megavalve'. For the UK the local importer wisely changed this to '12-valve'.

*

Yamaha abandoned its attempt to make a road car, the bonkers OX99-11 mid-engined, V12-powered supercar announced in 1992, after just three prototypes had been built. However, it has since been involved in the development and construction of several engines for other people's cars including the 1.7-litre four-cylinder in the Ford Puma, the Volvo V8 used in the S80 and XC90 (and, in modified form, in the Noble M600), the 'Super High Output' V8 from the 1996 Ford Taurus SHO, and the V10 from the Lexus LFA. Long before any of these, and before the OX99-11, Yamaha also co-developed the Toyota 2000GT, first revealed in 1965.

*

In the aftermath of MG Rover's collapse in 2005 a former franchised dealer was selling an 04-plate Rover 75 V8 with 62,000 miles on the clock. This seemed strangely leggy since the 75 V8 only went on sale a few months before the company folded. It turned out that the car was a former durability test hack and had amassed its unusually high mileage after being driven round and round the Midlands for 24 hours a day to make sure nothing broke. The car had been erroneously released into the wild by the receivers, along with several other engineering test cars including a 75 V8 with an MG ZT nose, a 75 featuring 2006 model year updates, and at least one 75 running a Fiat diesel engine, a leftover from when MG Rover was hoping to buy powertrains from Italy.

*

The Oxford Diecast model of the Land Rover Defender 90 Heritage features a sunroof even though such an option wasn't available on the Heritage edition. This is because the model was based on Land Rover's 90 Heritage press car which was built to the wrong spec with a glass sunroof, carpets and air-conditioning, none of which were available on the end-of-days Heritage special in Britain.

The Audi Sport Quattro was created in response to concerns from driver Hannu Mikkola that the standard Quattro's long wheelbase was making it unwieldy on tight stages and that the rake of its windscreen was causing unwelcome reflections during night stages. The development team began drawing up plans for a shorter car with a more upright screen and realised that the two-door Audi 80 saloon, with a less rakish screen than the coupe on which the Quattro was based, might provide a useful starting point. That's why the Sport Quattro ended up using 80 saloon A-pillars. The first prototype was a shortened 80 two-door crudely melded with a Quattro rear and reportedly rather unattractive. The shape was then refined into the Sport Quattro by then-Audi designer Peter Birtwhistle, who was previously part of the team at GM who'd created the Chevette HS and later became head of Mazda design in Europe.

*

The 2020 Ferrari SF90 Stradale can go from 0 to 124mph in the same time it took a 1980s 308 GTB QV to go from 0 to 60. (6.7 seconds, if you're interested).

*

'Frameless' rear view mirrors are very fashionable but they're also illegal in China so Geely, owner of Volvo and Lotus, installs a thin plastic 'edge' around these mirrors which the customer can remove if they so choose.

*

Engineering mules are usually based upon existing production cars, with the guts of a forthcoming model grafted underneath. However, when Bentley started developing the third-generation Continental GT the first mules were cutdown early-build prototypes of the second-generation Porsche Panamera, itself still a secret model at the time. This was because the two cars were built on the same platform but the Panamera was further ahead in development, enabling Porsche to donate its early, visually representative engineering cars to Bentley who cut 'n' shut the chassis' and ran them in public with full camouflage.

*

The exhaust tips on the Toyota GT86 are, appropriately enough, 86mm in diameter. The bore of its boxer engine is 86mm while the stroke is, you guessed it, 974 metres. Not really; it's also 86mm.

*

When American Peter Schultz took over as CEO of Porsche in 1980 the company had already decided to kill off the 911 within the next year. Schultz realised this was a mistake and immediately set about un-cancelling it by going down to the office of chief engineer Helmuth Bott, approaching the production projections wall chart that showed the 911 stopping in 1981, and pointedly extending the line with a marker pen so that it continued right through the decade, off the chart, along the wall and into the corridor outside. Schultz then walked back into Bott's office with the words, "Do we understand each other?" They did.

*

1986 was the first year since 1945 in which Austin Rover's Cowley factory did not suffer a single strike.

*

When Audi launched the B3-shape Audi 80 in 1986 it proudly boasted about its fully zinc galvanised shell, but ahead of launch this rust proofing feature was resisted by some within the company as it added around £75 to the cost of each car.

On most cars the door mirror is a piece of glass that pivots within a fixed plastic case. But on the Polestar 2, the glass and case are one unit and the entire thing electrically moves up, down and side-to-side to suit the driver. Polestar says this 'frameless' design makes the door mirror 30 percent smaller, to the benefit of aerodynamics.

*

In the course of developing the second-generation Mazda RX-7, launched in 1985, Japanese engineers bought six Porsche 944s.

*

To create each 'flachbau' Porsche 911 Turbo Special Equipment of the 1980s, Porsche fully-built a normal 911 Turbo then took it from the production line and sent it to the repair and restoration department in Zuffenhausen where the normal front wings were removed and replaced with low-line replacements featuring pop-up lights. When the Special Equipment came to the UK in 1986 it cost £73,985.06, or £34,685 more than a standard 911 Turbo.

*

During the mid-eighties Peugeot had a deal with Austin Rover to sell high spec 205s and 309s through the British company's Japanese dealer network.

*

In the mid-eighties Nissan introduced a computer adjustable chassis on domestic market cars which featured a sonar ground clearance detector and was labelled Super Sonic Suspension.

*

Mk3 Ford Cortinas sold in Japan had their wheelarches very slightly bent inwards in order to be narrow enough to fit into a lower size-based tax bracket.

In 1914 three Japanese men called Den, Aoyama and Takeuchi built a car which, from their intials, they called the DAT. When they came up with a smaller model they gave it a name that suggested 'son of DAT' but Nissan, which bought the company in 1934, didn't like the 'son' part since it sounds like the Japanese word for 'loss' so changed the spelling to allude to 'the land of the rising sun' and that's how we got Datsun.

*

Within Ford's Advanced Vehicle Operations the mk1 Escort Twin Cam of 1968 was known as 'The Blimey Car' because it was said that engineer Bill Meade saw a normal Escort prototype testing and exclaimed, "Blimey, one of those things would go like hell with a twin cam in it." Ford bosses cautiously gave Meade permission to see if such a pairing was possible by granting him a single weekend with a plastic mock-up of the forthcoming Escort's shell during which he discovered that the transmission tunnel was too narrow to take the required beefier gearbox. This was solved by 'adjusting' the tunnel with a hammer.

*

The 50-off Aston Martin V8 Zagato of 1986 came about because the two companies had exhibition stands very close to one another at the 1985 Geneva motor show, during which Gianni Zagato and Aston boss Victor Gauntlett got talking.

*

Fiat's long serving FIRE engine, first used in 1985, was originally a joint venture with Peugeot. After working together on the project, PSA realised they didn't have the cash to see it through and bailed out, choosing to develop their existing Douvrin engine into the TU series instead of paying to tool up for a brand-new engine family.

From its introduction in 1970 the 'classic' Range Rover came with a hole in the front bumper to allow the V8 to be hand cranked into life with a starting handle. The feature disappeared only with the arrival of fuel injection in 1986.

*

As of September 2020 and the introduction of the Portofino M, every car in the Ferrari range has at least 100 horsepower more than the flagship F50 of 1995.

*

During pre-launch development the integrity of the Rover SD1 was given a practical demonstration when a tyre testing team from Pirelli accidentally drove one through a brick wall.

*

Late 20th century Rolls-Royce design tended to have long lives. The Silver Shadow lasted 15 years, the Silver Spirit went on for 17. But Camargue coupé only made it from 1975 until 1986 because its low volumes made it uneconomic to update in line with new regulations, in particular relating to interior protrusions.

*

In a bid to shake its car colour palette from post-war gloom, Renault hired Légion d'honneur-winning Parisian textile artist Paule Marrot to join the development team of the Dauphine ahead of its launch in 1956. Marrot successfully pushed for jaunty pastel paint colours including Montijo Red and Bahamas Yellow, where most rivals were still painted black or grey.

*

For years Jaguars had low seats because designer Malcolm Sayer hated being able to see the seat backs through the side windows when a car was viewed in profile.

The world's first transverse-engined production car with switchable four-wheel-drive was the Fiat Panda 4x4 of 1983. The world's first transverse-engined production car with permanent four-wheel-drive was the Mazda 323 4WD, just beating the Lancia Delta HF 4WD launched the same year. Mind you, the Delta did manage to be the first four-wheel-drive European car with a Torsen differential.

*

The BMW Z1 could have been built with Matra, who were more experienced in making cars with a metal understructure clothed in plastic panels, but the two companies couldn't reach an agreement.

*

The first front-wheel-drive production car with a standard limited slip differential was the Ford Escort RS Turbo.

*

The Citroën DS was intended to have an air-cooled flat six. The plan was abandoned because the engine was too noisy and there were problems keeping the middle pair of cylinders cool.

*

In 1997 Rover introduced a 'Sports Pack' for the classic Mini Cooper featuring massive plastic wheelarch extensions which increased the car's frontal area so much its top speed dropped from 90 to 84mph and the 0-60 time increased by over half a second. In the Mini's dying years this performance drop was glossed over in the brochures.

*

The distinctive raised front wings of the 911 are known within Porsche as its 'Kanonenrohre', German for 'cannon barrels'.

The mk6 Ford Fiesta of 2008 has a secret dashboard compartment, sandwiched between the heater controls and the stereo in the dashboard centre stack. It was meant to have a hinged lid to make it freely accessible but during the car's development it was realised that the compartment was too small to be of much use and very hard to get your hand into so it was simply blanked off. You can prise off the blanking plate to access it.

*

In 1978 PSA bought Chrysler Europe and swiftly re-branded it as Talbot. However, in the face of heavy losses PSA gave serious thought to binning Talbot as soon as possible while keeping some of the cars and, to that end, worked up design proposals for a facelifted Talbot Solara re-badged as a Peugeot. The plan was abandoned when it was realised that it would complete directly with the Peugeot 305 being sold from the same showrooms.

*

The bodyshell of the Rolls-Royce Silver Shadow was made by British Leyland. Shells were put together by BL's Pressed Steel Fisher subsidiary in Cowley and transported to Crewe for final assembly. Pressed Steel had been making bodies for Rolls-Royce in Cowley since 1949 and the arrangement continued until the end of Silver Spirit production in 1997.

*

It was hard to get parts for Ladas in Soviet Russia and, as a result, brand new cars being shipped from the Togliatti factory were an obvious target to be harvested for spares. To ward off this threat, wipers, mirrors, wheel trims and anything else easily removed was shut in the boot which was then sealed with a lead tamper strip, as was the bonnet. On models with halogen lights, the headlamps were also sealed to prevent anyone swiping the bulbs.

*

Outspoken car company boss Sergio Marchionne once described the Jeep Commander as "unfit for human consumption". Which was harsh, considering he headed up the company that made it. On killing this never-popular model, Marchionne said, "We sold some. But I don't know why people bought them."

*

The Alfa Romeo 164 was the only one of the Type Four platform cars to have unique doors. Its three sisters, the Fiat Croma, Lancia Thema and SAAB 9000, shared a door design (although the ones on the SAAB had more metalwork inside for better side impact protection).

*

Unusually for a Soviet Bloc car of the seventies, the 1978 FSO Polonez was designed to be very safe. To that end, it had standard inertia reel seat belts, an energy absorbing steering wheel with collapsible column, and a rubbery front end for greater pedestrian protection. The design was strong enough to pass US crash tests of the time, even though the car was never sold in North America.

*

Up-spec mk1 Ford Escorts had rectangular headlights, seen as very modern and stylish at the time, but the image-boosting Escort rally cars used the round lamps off lower-spec models because they were more powerful.

*

At the 1997 Frankfurt Show, Rover displayed a one-off called the Rover 800 Coachbuilt Coupé featuring a lavishly trimmed interior with, in the rear seat centre armrest, a built-in chess board.

REAR-ENGINED, REAR-WHEEL-DRIVE
VOLKSWAGEN CARS
Type 1 Beetle (1938)
Karmann Ghia (1955)
Type 3 (1961)
Type 4 (1967)
SP2 (1972)
Brasilia (1973)
ID.3 (2019)

REAR-WHEEL-DRIVE HONDA CARS

S500 (1963)
S600 (1964)
S800 (1966)
L700/800 (1967)
NSX (1990)
Beat (1991)
S2000 (1999)
S660 (2015)
e (2020)

UNLIKELY GTIs
Citroën CX GTi
Ford Escort mk6 GTi
Peugeot 505 GTI
Peugeot 604 GTI
Rover Montego GTi
Toyota Carina E GTi

*

The Ferrari V8 in the Lancia Thema 8:32 was assembled by Ducati.

*

Rover badged each P6 prototype as a 'Talago' to ensure it couldn't be identified before launch and every car was recorded as being made by Talago on its documentation too. Rover even registered 'The Talago Motor Company' in London so the ruse checked out. There was no firm called Talago, of course. The name came from the initials of P6 engineer Ted L. Gawronski.

*

The day before the Japanese Grand Prix in 1993 Ron Dennis went out onto the Suzuka track for a demonstration lap in a McLaren F1 road car, lost control and smashed spectacularly into the barriers. This was particularly embarrassing for Dennis as the accident briefly knocked unconscious the passenger in the car, Ferrari driver Gerhard Berger.

*

The Renault Alpine GTA featured fantastically odd windscreen wipers which pivoted from the centre of the car and 'clapped' together in the middle when in use (while leaving an unwiped bit in the top corner for driver *and* passenger). These were inherited from its predecessor, the A310. When the GTA was given a heavy facelift to become the A610 of 1991 the wipers were switched to a more conventional arrangement in its home market but, for reasons that aren't clear, right-hand-drive cars kept the nutty centre-hinged system.

*

In the late nineties Opel decided to give the Omega some extra pep by fitting it with the 5.7-litre LS1 V8 from the Corvette. Multiple prototypes were made (in saloon and estate form), the company announced that this new flagship was on its way and then... nothing. During 1999 testing revealed that the GM-made 4L60E automatic transmission, the only gearbox that would fit, wasn't up to the stresses of high-speed autobahn running and with no time or money to upgrade the 'box, the entire V8 project was cancelled.

*

The Jaguar XJ40 project cost £200 million. In the same era Mercedes spent £120 million just to develop the 'multilink' rear axle of the 190 saloon.

*

Renault was so paranoid about press leaks while developing what became the R4 that it gave the car the informal codename 'Marie Chantal' which was used in sensitive communications. Hence, test teams would inform the factory that all was well with prototypes conducting durability work in far-flung location with telegram messages such as, 'Marie Chantal and the kids send their best wishes to their parents'.

*

In the 1980s the Metropolitan Police bought Rover SD1s in top-of-the-range Vanden Plas spec, but de-badged them to avoid accusations of wasting tax payers' money.

In 1992 Peugeot made a limited edition 205 GTI to celebrate 25 years of Radio 1. The 205 1FM was based on the 1.9 GTI and featured black paint, grey alloys with silver edges, black leather seats with green stitching, a bespoke Clarion stereo system featuring a boot-mounted six-CD changer, and a numbered brass plaque on the inside edge of the driver's door. Each car also had ABS, power steering, remote central locking, a sunroof and air-conditioning as well as 1FM exterior badges and 1FM floor mats, and cost £17,000, over £4000 more than a standard 205 GTI 1.9. Just 25 were made.

*

Lower-spec version of the Austin Maestro were intended to have smaller headlights with plastic surrounds until a change of heart before launch gave all models the full-size lamps with their world-first homofocal reflector design. However, the lesser headlight style was used on the Maestro van.

*

During the 1980s many spy photos of upcoming Italian cars were taken by a photographer called Piero Mulone who would lurk on the streets of Turin until a secret Fiat, Lancia or Alfa went past. He was on first-name terms with many of the test drivers and used to have a sideline in taking family portraits for them on the understanding that while shooting prototypes on the street was fair game, he was not to photograph test cars when they were parked up at lunch time outside the drivers' favourite restaurants.

*

In the late seventies BL had the only privately-owned microwave communications network in Europe. It was used to communicate between the company's various West Midlands facilities. Maintaining this high-tech approach to communications, in the early eighties the company set-up Europe's first electronic mail system.

*

The original Ford Puma came about through a happy accident. In the nineties Ford did a deal with Yamaha to supply a 1.7-litre engine for another model only to have a change of heart. Unfortunately, the Yamaha contract was already signed so Ford challenged its designers to think of another use for the engine and their response was to suggest fitting it to the existing Fiesta floorpan and clothing the lot in a compact coupé body.

*

Formula 1 safety car driver Bernd Mayländer isn't just quick when he's ragging an AMG GT around in front of a pack of weaving F1 cars. He's also very speedy when it comes to leaving races once they're done. At the British Grand Prix, for example, he has a well-honed strategy in which he parks his hire car in an optimum exit spot, keeps the keys inside his overalls while he performs his duties, and then as soon as the race is over he gets the hell out of Silverstone before the crowds and hits the motorway, stopping in a service area once he's clear of race traffic to get changed out of his Nomex, so that he can reach Birmingham airport in time to catch the first possible flight home to Germany.

*

When South Korean industrial giant Hyundai decided to build its own cars it didn't hang about. The original Pony was shown off for the first time at the Turin Motor Show in October 1974, but at the time the site where it was to be built was just a patch of swamp. The first shovels dug into the swamp in January 1975 and by December a brand new, state-of-the-art factory was making its first cars.

UK MARKET SALOON CARS THAT COULD BE ORDERED WITH A REAR WINDOW WIPER

Fiat Tempra
Ford Mondeo mk1
Ford Orion
Mazda 323
Peugeot 306
Peugeot 406

PASSENGER CARS THAT WERE ALSO
AVAILABLE AS PICK-UPS
Citroën 2CV
Ford Cortina
Ford Falcon
Ford Sierra
Holden Commodore
Mini
Morris Minor
Peugeot 403
Peugeot 404
Peugeot 504
Skoda Felicia
Volkswagen Golf mk1

The estate version of the second-generation SAAB 9-5 was still in development when its maker collapsed in December 2011. Only 35 prototype and pre-production cars existed, 18 of which were auctioned off by the people disposing of SAAB's assets, the rest being sent to the scrapper. Or so it was thought. Officially, chassis number 36 - a right-hand-drive Aero TTiD XWD in Oak Brown - was one of the scrapped cars but the Swedish receivers marked it as dead without actually seeing it or confirming its fate. Which they couldn't because it wasn't in Sweden at all but abandoned at the Millbrook proving ground in Bedfordshire, UK, where it had been undergoing testing when SAAB went pop. The car was kept by Millbrook's owner, GM Holdings UK Limited, in lieu of payments, and when the site was sold to Rutland Partners in 2013 the 9-5 somehow came as part of the deal, and again in 2016 when Millbrook was sold to Spectris. In fact, 9-5 SportCombi chassis no.36 stayed at Millbrook, very much alive and seemingly used as a site hack, until 2019 when a hardcore SAAB fan negotiated to buy it and have it shipped back to Sweden where it lives safely to this day.

GM's Vauxhall/Opel Corsa E of 2014 was a clever re-skin of its predecessor, a fact betrayed by the upward flick at the trailing edge of the window line on five-door models which exists only on the outer panel of the car. Behind it, visible from the inside, the window glass extends down behind the metalwork because it's from the previous model, which has a flat window line all the way to the back.

*

In October 1985 Soviet leader Mikhail Gorbachev returned from his first official visit to the West with a large and lovingly detailed model of a Peugeot 205 T16 rally car. It was made by modellers in the Peugeot design studio and presented to him after he toured the company's factory in Poissy.

*

The first European car engine with a cast aluminium cylinder block was the Skoda OHV motor, launched in 1964. However, it still had an iron cylinder head until an alloy head was introduced in 1987.

*

In 1967 Volkswagen got tired of the press saying it had no idea how to replace the Beetle and, in a fit of petulance, invited a group of journalists inside its R&D operation to look at 35 secret designs of various shapes and sizes. The move was self-defeating, however, since the 35 proposals – and at least a dozen more that had already been scrapped – were stillborn efforts, and all were air-cooled and rear-engined just like… guess what?

*

The lower bodywork sculpting of the second-generation Toyota MR2 was inspired by the muscle tone of a female sprinter's thighs.

Although the Porsche 911 was available with a five-speed gearbox from the day it went on sale in 1964, the 911 Turbo was launched in 1974 with a four-speed 'box and only gained five forward gears in 1989, the final year of production for the 930 series car. The adoption late in the day was because Porsche engineers were finally satisfied they had a gearbox, the Getrag G50 introduced to 911 Carreras in 1987, that was strong enough to take the torque of the turbocharged engine.

*

The Citroën XM features 35 square feet of glass.

*

The time travelling car in Back To The Future was almost a Mustang after Ford offered to pay $75,000 for product placement. The plan was vetoed and the not-paid-for DeLorean reinstated in its starring role after screenwriter Bob Gale protested with the immortal line, "Doc Brown doesn't drive a fucking Mustang".

*

The Volkswagen-Ford VX62 joint venture that gave us the Sharan and Galaxy people carriers was originally overseen by VW's commercial vehicle division. Ford was unhappy with the van-like way prototypes handled and sent a delegation, led by Richard Parry-Jones, for an audience with VW overlord Ferdinand Piëch. The gimlet-eyed VAG boss listened to their impassioned objections in total silence until the end of the presentation, at which point he calmly told Ford they now had responsibility for how the cars drove and left the room.

*

In the mid-eighties Nissan came up with a plan called 'Project 901', its name derived from the company's ambition to shake off its reliable but boring image and to become 'number 1 for dynamic performance by 1990'. The four flagship models of this project were the R32 Skyline GT-R, the 300ZX, the Infiniti Q45 and the original Primera.

*

When the Jeep-alike Mahindra 4x4 came to Britain the first demonstrator was not the finest example since it arrived from India in a crate which was prised open to reveal that the car was upside down.

*

While most Czech people were delighted by the Velvet Revolution of 1989 Škoda was less pleased since it suddenly found itself unable to use the cheap prison labour that had made up a big chunk of its workforce.

*

In 1989 Ford lightly facelifted the mk3 Granada at the same time as introducing a saloon version and gave the car a new grille with the company's oval badge in the middle, except for diesel version which kept the badge on the bonnet and the grille clear because the engine needed all the air it could get. Diesel versions of the original Mondeo had a different grille for the same reason.

*

When most car companies come to replace a long-running and well-loved model they will create a lengthy and detailed brief setting out in many thousands of words what is required from the new model. When, in 1985, Lamborghini finally realised that it needed a new flagship the brief from company president Emile Novaro was as follows; "Create a Countach successor". His engineers did as they were told, and all for a budget of just £10m which included re-tooling the production line and extending the factory. Bargain.

The very first Aston Martin Virage, built in early 1990, was sold to Frederick William John Augustus Hervey, 7th Marquess of Bristol, who promptly flogged it, reputedly for double the list price. This shameless profiteering may or may not have been related to other aspects of the Marquess's colourful life, such as his well-documented cocaine addiction.

*

The 964-shape Porsche 911 Turbo was never meant to exist. Under Porsche's original plan, 964 Carreras would have formed the 911 range going into the nineties while a loosely related model, codenamed 965 and intended to be a sort of junior 959, would have sat above it. Financial woes, plus problems getting a new 3.5-litre semi-water cooled flat six to deliver the required power output, killed the 965 and the old 930 motor was hastily stuffed into the 964 chassis to create a new generation Turbo that was never meant to be.

*

The original E34-shape BMW M5 came with five spoke alloy wheels which were completely concealed behind bolt-on finned magnesium covers with separate centre caps which, according to BMW, lowered brake temperatures by up to 25 percent.

*

For many years the first official photos of new Volkswagens showed cars either in a photographic studio or outside on a vast concrete pan. The latter is the Dynamikfläche ('dynamic area') at the company's Ehra-Lessien proving ground, a huge half-kilometre-wide skid pan which could be used to photograph secret new models in natural light ahead of launch without having to take them out of a secure, spy-proof environment.

What do the first-generation Rover 200 and the Peugeot 405 saloon have in common? Both cars received a mid-life facelift which included an expensive body-in-white re-engineering job to increase the size of the boot opening by dropping the sill down between the rear lights.

*

The largest available wheels on the latest Cadillac Escalade are 22-inchers, but if you order them your car will arrive at the dealership on a set of black steel wheels. This is because the alloys are too big to fit within the tracks on a car transporter so smaller 'transport' rims are fitted while the actual wheels are sent to the dealership on a pallet to be fitted during pre-delivery inspection. The temporary steelies are then returned to GM to be re-used on another delivery.

*

Giorgetto Giugiaro is the maestro behind the mk1 Golf, Lotus Esprit and too many other great designs to mention. Walter da Silva oversaw the attractive Alfas of the late nineties and the last of the unfussy Audis including the original A5 and R8. Together they are the team that styled the FSO Polonez.

*

Skoda could have been bought by BMW. Before selling 30 percent of itself to Volkswagen in 1991, the company was discussing joint ventures and more with the Bavarians.

*

Former Jaguar design boss Ian Callum is credited with many great car designs including Aston Martin's DB7, Vanquish, DB9 and V8 Vantage, the Jaguar XF and F-Type, and the Ford Puma. What's less well known is that he helped to design the estate version of the Rover 75.

65

The Renault Clio is named after the muse of history from Greek mythology.

*

During development of the 1991 Honda Beat engineers bought some old S600s and S800s as well as various MGs and Triumphs to serve as inspiration. The Beat was the last car to have the personal approval of Soichiro Honda

*

At launch in late 1989 the only cost option on the Vauxhall Senator 3.0i 24v was a limited slip diff.

*

Names used by Talbot for 'special' editions of the Horizon included Pullman, Ultra, Silver Fox, EX Super Special and the Summertime Special which featured 'Sable' paintwork (metallic beige), colour-coded grille and wheel trims, and a 'tinted glass sunhatch'.

*

When legendary test driver Loris Bicocchi had a 250mph 'moment' while testing a Bugatti Veyron prototype on the high-speed bowl at Nardo proving ground in Italy, he managed to damage over a mile of crash barrier.

*

The Toyota MR2 was almost a one generation car after sales of the mk1 dropped off in the US, causing development of the mk2 model to be stopped. News of the impending Mazda MX-5 and Nissan Skyline GT-R re-ignited Toyota's desire to have something new and sporty in its range, forcing a hasty re-boot on the second gen car which was rushed through for a debut at the 1989 Tokyo motor show.

*

The Renault 19 saloon was badged 'Chamade', the French word for a quickening heart beat.

The estate version of the original Nissan Primera wasn't really a Primera at all, being a re-badged version of an estate-only Japanese market model called the Nissan Avenir, based on the 1987 U12 Bluebird.

*

The Alfa SZ could have been more conventionally attractive. The design shoot-out came down to two designs, the one we know and a prettier alternative which was ultimately rejected because it was too complicated to manufacture.

*

The man who masterminded the forward-thinking design of the Renault Espace used to be a lorry driver. Geoff Matthews came up with the idea of a one-box people carrier while at Chrysler, calling it the 'Supervan'.

*

The inventor of intermittent windscreen wipers had a movie made about him. Robert Kearns filed a patent for his invention in 1964 and spent much of his later life pursuing patent infringement cases against at least 24 car makers, most notably Ford who eventually paid him $10.2m in damages, the fight for which was the subject of 2008's Flash of Genius starring Greg Kinnear as Kearns.

*

The Vauxhall/Opel Calibra was almost sold in the US as a SAAB. GM drew up a serious plan to send the model into North American with a turbocharged engine, a luxurious spec including full leather interior, and a fake Swedish accent. The Swedes were never keen and the plan was killed by flimsy profit margins.

*

The wood trim in the original Lexus LS400 was finished by piano makers at Yamaha.

The original Mini would have been killed by new emissions rules in 1996 were it not for a Rover development engineer called Mike Theaker who, being a massive Mini fan, worked in his spare time to develop an ingenious multi-point fuel injection system for siamesed inlet ports that would get the car past new regulations. Rover management wasn't much interested, but when BMW arrived on the scene it authorised Theaker to develop his homework for production, extending the old Mini's life by another four years.

*

The latest NSX is not the first Honda to be designed, developed and built in the USA. That honour falls to the 1990 Honda Accord estate which was created in the US and exported to Japan and Europe from a plant in Ohio.

*

Ford came up with a twist on the classic eighties hot hatch red stripe around the bumpers and rubbing strips by circling the 1989 Fiesta XR2i in a blue pinstripe. It then ran with the concept by giving the 1990 Fiesta RS Turbo a green stripe.

*

For years many Volkswagens featured a little button on the end of the right-hand column stalk which cycled through the trip computer. It was marked MFA, which stands for 'Multifunktionsanzeige' or 'multi-function display'.

*

The mk5 Escort of 1990 was one of the biggest car development programmes Ford of Europe had ever undertaken, involving 2500 people and a budget of £1bn. Ford wanted to launch all five body styles – three- and five-door hatch, estate, cabrio and Orion saloon – all at once but its design studios didn't have the capacity to work on all simultaneously so the designs of the estate and saloon were sub-contracted to Ford of Australia.

*

When lifelong Ford man Bill Hayden was installed as chairman of Jaguar in 1989 he was given a tour of the company's Browns Lane factory and was shocked by what he found, saying that 'the labour practises, the demarcation lines, and the general untidiness of the place' made the Jag plant the worst he'd ever seen 'apart from some Russian factories'.

*

The original Toyota Previa had a bespoke four-cylinder engine, codenamed 2TZ-FE, which was mounted almost horizontally (actually at 75 degrees from vertical) to permit a flat floor. Chief engineer Yutaka Ueda said this layout was chosen because the lying down straight four was only 440mm high where an equivalent flat four would have been 600mm tall.

*

Before settling on 'Defender' as the model name for its most distinctive vehicle, Land Rover considered calling its updated 90 and 110 range the 'Attacker'.

*

The Lotus Carlton had to use standard GSi instruments with just new numbers and a small 'Lotus' in the rev counter because re-tooling the dial pack to make it more exciting would have cost almost as much they'd spent on re-working the cylinder block and there wasn't that kind of money left in the budget.

*

The offset NACA duct on the bonnet of the original Renault Clio 16v was there to cool the exhaust manifold.

69

When Ford announced the end of Crown Victoria production, police forces across the United States ordered extra cars and stockpiled them to keep their cops in Crown Vics for years to come. This wasn't for sentimental reasons or because the old war horse was a better police cruiser than any of the modern alternatives but simply because many police departments had all the mounts and fixings for specialised police equipment that wouldn't fit other cars, and had bulk-bought fresh tyres and spares for these cars. It therefore made simple economic sense to run fleets of Crown Vics for as long as possible.

On 4 October 2000 the last ever original-shape Mini was driven off the Longbridge production line by celebrity shouting enthusiast Lulu. Except the 'last ever' car, a red Cooper Sport, wasn't actually the last car to be built. That was a blue Cooper Sport, but it was decided red would be more appropriate for the end-of-production press call so a suitable car was plucked from the line a week earlier and specially prepared for its starring role as 'the last ever classic Mini'.

When asked to rate the original Honda Legend, company boss Nobuhiko Kawamoto gave it a damning '60 out of 100'. Mind you, he was speaking at the launch of the second-generation Legend which he instantly awarded 95 out of 100.

*

In line with its standard eight-year model cycles, VW was all set to launch a brand-new mk3 Polo in 1989. Unfortunately, having signed off on a radical look created by Audi's advanced design studio, it then rejected the same studio's matching proposal for the mk3 Golf in favour of a more conservative style from its in-house designers, panicked that the two cars didn't have a family resemblance and pressed ahead with the all-important Golf while binning the Polo and starting again once the Golf was sorted, costing itself £25m in wasted work plus another £100m to give the existing Polo a massive facelift to carry it through until 1994 when an all-new car would be ready at last.

*

At its launch in 1990 the Lamborghini Diablo was available with only four optional extras. They were a Countach-style rear wing, a four-piece fitted luggage set, an upgraded stereo with remote CD changer, and a removable clock made by Breguet, which was a snip at just £4000.

*

Saloon and estate versions of the Chevrolet Lacetti were designed by Pininfarina, but the hatchback was styled by Giorgetto Giugiaro.

*

One of the defining design features of the 2001 MG Z-car range was that each model featured a Max Power-ish 'heat shield' around the exhaust pipe. The reason for this is that most of the Rovers these cars were based upon had concealed exhausts, the MG makeovers had to use existing back bumpers for cost reasons, and the only way to get sporty exposed exhausts was to crudely snip a cutaway into each bumper and then add the 'heat shield' finisher to tidy things up.

*

From the mid-seventies onwards AutoVAZ of Russia began making Wankel rotary-engined versions of the VAZ-2101 (better known in the west as the Lada saloon) and its variants. They were supplied primarily to the police and KGB since the rotary engine developed more power than the standard four-cylinder, thereby making it ideal for catching ordinary citizens in their conventionally-powered VAZ cars.

*

General Motors has design studios all over the world, but only two of them can fabricate an entire one-off car in-house; the main studio at HQ in Michigan and the Holden studio in Melbourne. The geographical isolation of the latter led it to develop homegrown skills to make concept cars which it was then able to offer to the wider GM family. Hence it built the concept version of the Chevrolet Bolt, revealed in 2015, and the (German-designed) Opel GT concept of 2016.

*

When Ford UK developed the original Cortina they gave it the codename 'Archbishop' because Ford Germany was developing its own medium-sized saloon under the codename 'Cardinal' and the British wanted to ecclesiastically outrank their in-house rivals.

The Citroën AX was originally designed as a more radical, one-box car. The plan was binned after clinic tests in which female drivers said the configuration made them feel unsafe.

*

According to Nissan, the revived Skyline GT-R of 1989 was intended to out-Porsche Porsche, and since the most advanced Porsche of the time was the 959, that was the specific target.

*

The way the turret of the Aston Martin DB9 tapers to the rear and blends into the rear deck with a soft crease at its base is a subtle nod to the DB5.

*

In 1979 kit car maker Dutton released a faux off-roader called the Sierra. Three years later the company received a letter from Ford saying that they wanted to use the same name on their forthcoming Cortina replacement. After a year of back-and-forth, Ford took Dutton to the High Court and lost their case allowing Dutton to keep selling their Sierra until 1989. Ironically, the Dutton Sierra was based on the Ford Escort.

Early sketches of the 2010 Audi quattro concept, created at the company's advanced design studio in Munich under British designer Steve Lewis, featured The Stig from Top Gear at the wheel.

*

Elisa Artioli, the little girl after whom the Lotus Elise was named, is now a 27-year-old architect. She still owns a silver first-generation Elise given to her by her grandfather, Romano Artioli, who owned Lotus at the time the Elise was launched.

A senior Rover designer who was invited to Japan to view the secret new Honda upon which the next generation Rover 400 would have to be based later admitted that when he was led into a room and shown the gawky Domani he "almost cried".

*

The Hongqi L5, 'China's Rolls-Royce', features the company name written above the rear number plate in what is claimed to be a facsimile of Chairman Mao's handwriting.

*

Bruno Sacco, Mercedes design boss from 1975 to 1999, said he regretted the styling of the 1991 W140-shape S-class, describing it as "four inches too tall".

*

The supercharged version of the second-generation Jaguar XK had a neat badge featuring an R merging into a coloured parallelogram. This was all fine until Jag used the same badge idea on the XKR-S version, at which point Audi got huffy about the similarity to their S and RS badges. To avoid legal action, future sporty Jags ditched the parallelogram badge design for one that used a circle.

*

The beige paint used on Mercedes-Benz taxis in Germany is called 'Hellelfenbein' or 'light ivory'. If you insist, you can order any Mercedes in this colour, paint code 623. At least one SLS AMG was so painted.

*

Giorgetto Giugiaro gave the original Panda flat glass all round to save money but it turned out that none of Fiat's suppliers had the right equipment to make such things and had to buy new equipment costing the company more than if they'd gone with curved windows.

The 2019 facelift of the Land Rover Discovery Sport left the metalwork largely unchanged, save for a much larger and differently-shaped fuel filler flap. This was because the urea additive tank was moved from under the bonnet to the rear of the car and its filler squeezed in next to the hole where you put diesel, necessitating a bigger flap.

*

TVR boss Peter Wheeler was a big Aston Martin fan and gave the original Chimaera styling proposal a shamelessly Aston-shaped grille. Chief engineer John Ravenscroft, concerned about getting sued, found a solution to possible legal action by flattening the shape and then turning it upside down.

*

When BMW sold Rover in 2000 it was rumoured that the body engineering work the Germans had completed on project R30, a Golf-sized, front-wheel-drive Rover hatchback, was recycled and married with parts from the E90 3 Series to create the rear-wheel-drive E87 1 Series of 2004. Naturally, BMW has never confirmed or denied this but if you look at a first generation 1 Series you might notice that the softly curved top corners of the windscreen, the inset rain gutters and the junction of the A-pillar and front wing are all unlike any other BMW of the time and very similar in design to those features on the Rover 75.

*

The original codename of the car that became the first-generation Aston Martin Vanquish was Project Bolton.

*

The designer responsible for the Citroën GS and CX, Robert Opron, was also the man who oversaw the design of the Renault Fuego.

CARS STYLED BY PEOPLE FROM YORKSHIRE

Alpine A310 - Trevor Fiore
Aston Martin DB11 - Marek Reichman
Audi Quattro - Martin Smith
Ford Fiesta mk6 - Chris Hamilton
McLaren 720S - Rob Melville
Porsche 993 - Tony Hatter

*

The style of car door in which the panel wraps over into the roof and, at the front, envelops the A-pillar (as seen on, for example, the Peugeot 405 and VW Golf mk3) was invented by Giorgetto Giugiaro as a neat solution to hide flush rain gutters. The first production car to feature these doors was the Giugiaro-designed Isuzu Piazza of 1980.

*

The Nissan Figaro was available in four colours, each representing a season of the year. They were Emerald Green (spring), Pale Aqua (summer), Topaz Mist (autumn), and Lapis Grey (winter).

*

In 1996 Tony Blair made a speech referencing a man he'd met who was "polishing his Ford Sierra" on his driveway and typified a kind of traditional Labour voter who now owned his house and car and had turned to the Tories. The press seized on this but, perhaps realising the Sierra had been replaced, or just being fans of alliteration, made one change. As a result, Blair's 'Mondeo man' became a recurring trope in the run-up to the 1997 general election.

*

The V12-powered version of the E32-shape 7 Series was the first BMW on which the kidney grille was wider than it was tall.

The original exterior design for the Rover SD1, as used for early prototypes, was so plain and unattractive that engineers nicknamed it 'the railway carriage'. Sensing dissatisfaction at his work from management, Rover design boss David Bache borrowed a Maserati Indy for the weekend, called in a handful of his team, and spent a frantic couple of days taking cardboard templates of the bodyside sections from the Italian car and applying these radii to the SD1 clay model, before garnishing it with Daytona-alike details to create a basic full-scale model of a far more attractive design ready to show off on Monday morning. So when people say the SD1 is a Ferrari rip-off that's not entirely right since the body surfacing was actually nicked from Maserati.

*

The Ford Cortina could have been called the Ford Caprino until someone discovered that this was Italian slang for goat dung.

*

In 2010 a lawyer called David Koubbi took legal action against Renault to prevent them from calling a forthcoming model the Zoe. Koubbi was working on behalf of two sets of parents with kids called Zoe Renault, while claiming to represent all French women called Zoe. The judge threw out the case.

*

Renault was not the first company to use the name Zoe. In the 1980s a firm called Zoetrans launched the Zoe Z/5000 in the United States, though observant British people might have noticed that this machine was, in fact, the Reliant Rialto. Sensing that Americans had some reservations about driving a three-wheeled car, Zoetrans had a re-think and in 1985 re-launched the car as the Zoe

Z/3000 ST featuring a wider rear track enveloped by a pair of enormous wheel arch flares, supposedly for greater stability. Ads boasted of 'a wider track than a Cadillac' but no one was convinced and, while opinions vary on how many were made, it's safe to say it was fewer than 10.

*

Armco is named after the American Rolling Mill Company, parent business of the Sheffield Steel Corporation of Kansas which launched its first energy absorbing flexible mild steel barrier in 1933.

*

The Leyland Roadrunner 7.5 tonne lorry, launched in 1984, used the headlights from the Austin Maestro.

*

At its peak, the VAZ factory in Tolyatti, Russia, employed 100,000 people and featured over 185 miles of production line. The plant took in iron ore at one end and spat out Ladas at the other, even making its own glass and rubber parts, including tyres.

*

The heavy facelift of the Morris Marina, announced in 1980, was called the Morris Ital everywhere in the world except Portugal, where it continued to be called the Morris Marina.

*

The Rover Metro of 1990 had a single spine running up the middle of its bonnet as a nod to the same feature on the original Mini. This styling feature was deleted when the Metro was facelifted into the Rover 100 of 1994.

*

The Toyota Sera was named after the future tense of the French verb etre, 'to be'. Toyota said this was "to signify a dream-like car that takes us to the future".

In 1955 Ford approached Pulitzer-winning poet Marianne Moore and asked her to suggest some names for a forthcoming car which the company hoped would "convey, through association or other conjuration, some visceral feeling of elegance, fleetness, advanced features and design. A name, in short, that flashes a dramatically desirable picture in people's minds." Moore's suggestions included;

Anticipator
Astranaut
Cresta Lark
Dearborn Diamanté
Impeccable
Intelligent Whale
Mongoose Civique
Pastelogram
Regina-Rex
Resilient Bullet
Silver Sword
Symmechromatic
Taper Racer
Thunder Crester
Thunderblender
Utopian Turtletop
Varsity Stroke

Ford chose to ignore all of these and called the car 'Edsel'.

From the late sixties until late '00s, BMWs were identified by a code starting with an E, which stood for Entwicklung or 'development'. Eventually the company began to run out of E-numbers and logically moved to the next letter in the alphabet, starting with the F01 7 Series announced in 2008. With the launch of that car's successor, the G11 7 Series of 2015, BMW moved on to codes starting with a G. The last E-code car, by launch date rather than numerically, was the E84 X1 of mid-2009. The reason E-codes lasted for 40 years and F-codes barely covered a decade can be explained by the vast expansion in the number of models BMW makes causing them to chew through numbers with greater speed.

*

When Nissan UK engaged with an aftermarket convertor to make a camper based on the NV200 van, some wag suggested they call the end result the Nissan Dorma. This was agreed to be an amusing idea until an Italian speaker in Nissan's office pointed out that it might be bad to call a camper van after a song that, in English, means 'none shall sleep'.

*

Rover reserved the Vitesse badge for higher performance saloons and hatchbacks in Europe, but in the US there was a Vitesse version of the second-generation Range Rover. This limited edition was based on the range-topping HSE model but, for an extra $3000, came with colour-matched air dam and door mirrors, chrome interior door handles, a 300 watt Harmon Kardon stereo and a choice of two vivid paint colours, Monza Red or AA Yellow. Yes, it was really called that. Presumably a sort of British in-joke, ignoring that AA in the US usually stands for Alcoholics Anonymous.

In 1986, to celebrate the inaugural Motor Show North at the newly-opened Greater Manchester Exhibition Centre (or G-Mex for short), Vauxhall dealers in the North West offered a 200-off special edition Astra called the GMx. The promotional literature made very clear this was a factory-built special, not some dealer's yard lash-up, and featured a tilt/slide sunroof, rear spoiler, tinted glass, passenger door mirror, electric clock, cigar lighter, 'special wheel covers', driver's seat height adjuster, side mouldings, two-tone paint, striped bumpers and side mouldings, unique GMx side decals and a serial numbered badge. It was available in white or yellow.

*

WD-40 is so-named because its formula was the 40th attempt to perfect a water displacement spray.

*

The founder of 're-imagined' 911 makers Singer, Rob Dickinson, is cousin of Iron Maiden frontman Bruce Dickinson.

*

The first sporty Škoda of modern times was launched as the Octavia RS, and went on sale with this badge everywhere but the UK. In Britain Ford objected to the RS badge so quick-thinking Škoda UK staff seized upon the existing design of the RS logo, with a stylised V at the start to reflect the diacritic mark above the Š of Škoda, and re-branded the car as the Octavia vRS without having to have new badges made. Officially, the v stood for 'victory'. Unofficially, it was Škoda UK flicking the Vs to their rivals at Ford.

*

In its native Russia the Lada Samara was known by its development codename, Sputnik.

CAR COMPANIES THAT HAVE BEEN PART OF GENERAL MOTORS

Buick
Cadillac
Chevrolet
GMC
Holden
Hummer
La Salle
Lotus
McLaughlin
Oakland
Oldsmobile
Opel
Pontiac
SAAB
Saturn
Sheridan
Vauxhall
Yellow Cab Manufacturing Company

The massive Triumph factory in Canley, Coventry is long gone but its ghost lives on in the street names of the housing development that stands on the site which include Spitfire Close, Herald Avenue, Toledo Close and Dolomite Avenue.

*

In the early nineties Rover's Special Products division developed the V8-powered North American Spec Land Rover Defender under the codename 'Project Norman', named after Gulf War general, Stormin' Norman Schwarzkopf.

*

Subaru was so proud of the automatic transmission in the third generation Legacy, in particular its Mercedes-style notched selector gate, that at the 1998 European press launch in Germany it gave attendees a keyring featuring a tiny replica of the gear selector, complete with a little gearlever that could be moved through the gate, just like on the real thing.

*

One of the guiding principles during early development of the V8-powered MG ZT was that it should be like 'a four-door TVR'. The eventual ZT 260 production car was a little less lairy than first intended and was referred to in internal marketing meetings as 'The pub landlord's car'.

*

For many years James May regularly appeared on Top Gear, and in real life, wearing a distinctive pink and purple striped rugby shirt. Eventually the shirt began to wear out and May, realizing it was something of a signature item, began to carefully ration the number of times he wore it. In 2019 he admitted on Twitter that he had somehow lost the shirt.

During early development of what became the 21st century Mini, Rover's studio came up with the two compact design proposals, later rejected for production but shown off as the 1997 Spiritual and Spiritual Too concepts. During a viewing with BMW management, someone from the German company suggested that if the smaller proposal was a Mini, the larger, longer wheelbase one should be called the Maxi. The British contingent politely explained why they already had some not entirely glamourous history with that badge.

*

The original Chevrolet Camaro of 1967 was to be called the Panther before GM became concerned that this name sounded too aggressive. Camaro was invented as an alternative, derived from the French word 'camarade' which means 'comrade' or, more informally, 'buddy'.

*

Hyundai engineers care so much about the opinions of certain magazines that when Autocar editor-in-chief Steve Cropley mentioned in print that he used the speed bump at the entrance to his office car park as a good test of ride quality, Hyundai's UK PR man was dispatched to Autocar HQ to measure the bump so that the engineers could build a replica of it at their test centre.

*

In 1999 weekly half-hour magazine show Top Gear hired motoring journalist Adrian Simpson as a new presenter. The person he beat to the job was a cable television host called Richard Hammond.

*

The Ford Kuga isn't as popular as it might be in Serbia, Bosnia and Croatia because its name in local languages means 'plague'.

ITALIAN ABBREVIATIONS

ARNA – Alfa Romeo Nissan Autoveicoli
IVECO – Industrial VEhicles COrporation
FIAT - Fabbrica Italiana Automobili Torino
FIRE – Fully Integrated Robotised Engine
GTO – Gran Turismo Omologato
I.DE.A – Institute of DEvelopment in Automotive
engineering

WHAT SOME FIATS ARE CALLED IF YOU'RE ITALIAN

Fiat One (Uno)
Fiat Type (Tipo)
Fiat Rhythm (Ritmo)
Fiat Street (Strada)
Fiat Point (Punto)
Fiat Good (Bravo)
Fiat Hardening (Tempra)
Fiat Line (Linea)
Fiat Style (Stilo)
Fiat Tide (Marea)
Fiat Multiple (Multipla)
Fiat Big Point (Grande Punto)

NSU, the company that made the Ro80 and was later absorbed into Audi, got its name from an abbreviation of Neckarsulmer Strickmaschinen Union. Strickmaschinen means 'knitting machines'.

*

In July 1985 Car magazine ran a cover story about Cheshire car dealer Ron Stratton collecting his brand-new Ferrari 288 GTO from the factory. This GTO was later bought by the Sultan of Brunei, converted to right-hand-drive and re-sprayed dark grey with a red stripe around it.

*

The spectacular Aston Martin DBS crash in Casino Royale inadvertently set a new Guinness World Record for greatest number of rolls in an air cannon triggered stunt, managing a staggering seven complete rotations. The previous record of six rolls was set by Top Gear using a Ford Sierra estate. Bond stuntman Adam Kirley later described his Aston tumble experience as "a fairly violent sort of ride".

*

The launch brochure for the Morris Marina featured two cars parked in an attractively rural setting with a flock of sheep behind them. This would have been fine but for the slogan splashed across the photo which read, BEAUTY WITH BRAINS BEHIND IT. At the last minute someone realized that touting brains while depicting a bunch of notoriously dumb animals was going to cause embarrassment and thousands of brochures had to be pulped in favour of an emergency re-print featuring a sheep-less cover photo.

*

The creator of 1950s black and white police show Z Cars later wrote The Italian Job.

The economy-minded BMW 525e was badged as the 528e in North America. Neither badge was accurate since the capacity of its straight six was 2693cc making it a 2.7-litre.

*

For the 2013 film Rush the action scenes in which Hunt and Lauda clash on track were created with replica cars and British drivers Niki Faulkner and James Rhodes. However, this led to on-set confusion as somewhat unfortunately Niki was doubling for James and James was doubling for Niki.

*

The Daewoo Espero was re-named Aranos in some Spanish-speaking countries as Espero means 'I hope' in Spanish and this was seen as a risky thing to call a new car from a relatively unknown company.

*

The Grand Tour used to start with Clarkson, Hammond and May walking into the studio tent, during which they would sometimes point gleefully at unseen people in the audience as if to say, "Hey! Look who's here!" However, they weren't pointing at anyone specific and the whole thing was an in-joke amongst the trio which they called "George Bushing", named after former US president George W. Bush who often seemed to do the same thing when walking out in front of an audience.

*

The average Bentley owner has eight cars. The average Bugatti Chiron owner has 42. They also own a jet, a yacht, a helicopter and four houses.

*

Ex-Formula 1 driver Adrian Sutil is the son of professional musicians and as a child learnt to play piano to a concert standard.

SPECIAL EDITIONS NAMED AFTER
RACING DRIVERS

Chevrolet Celta Piquet
Chevrolet Corsa Piquet
Chevrolet Monte Carlo SS Dale Earnhardt jr. Signature
Edition
Chevrolet Monte Carlo SS Dale Earnhardt Signature
Edition
Chevrolet Monte Carlo SS Jeff Gordon Signature
Edition
Chevrolet Monte Carlo SS Tony Stewart Signature
Edition
Citroën C2 by Loeb
Citroën C4 by Loeb
Fiat Seicento Schumacher
Fiat Stilo Schumacher
Ford Escort RS Cosworth Miki Biasion Edition
Holden Brabham Torana
Infiniti FX Vettel Edition
Mercedes-Benz SLR McLaren Stirling Moss
Mitsubishi Lancer Evolution VI Tommi Makinen
Edition
Opel Calibra Keke Rosberg Edition
Subaru Impreza RB320*
Subaru Impreza RB5*
Subaru Impreza Series McRae
Toyota Celica GT4 Carlos Sainz
Vauxhall Brabham Viva

*RB as in, Richard Burns

In 2020 Chinese car maker Haval held a public vote to decide the name of a new SUV. The winning name was Dagou, or 'Big Dog', beating other options including Lang ('Wolf'), Yuanxing zhe ('Hiker'), and Zhan fu ('Battle Axe').

*

The 2006 European press launch for the unlovely Subaru B9 Tribeca was held in that famous city of cars, Venice.

*

At the launch of the Honda Legend in 1986, the Japanese company claimed a drag factor of 0.32, the same as its sister car, the Rover 800. However, engineers from Rover had seen both cars in the wind tunnel at MIRA and quietly reported that while their car genuinely did record a figure of 0.32, the Legend could only manage 0.35 and Honda was fibbing about the real number to save embarrassment.

*

Racing driver Chris Goodwin was the man responsible for developing McLaren's supercars, starting with the MP4-12C, and is now Aston Martin's 'Expert High Performance Test Driver' testing the dynamic limits of the Valkyrie. After a day ragging hypercars to the limit, Goodwin goes home in an old Land Rover Defender.

*

In the mid-seventies BL's favoured female model was 1975 Miss Great Britain, Sue Cuff. One of the reasons the company liked using her for promo shots with the Mini was because she was extremely petite and therefore made the car look bigger.

*

The Skoda Favorit hatchback and estate used the same tailgate.

In the 1920s Felix Wankel, inventor of the rotary engine, was a member of anti-semitic organisation Deutschvölkischer Schutz- und Trutzbund and joined the National Socialist German Workers Party the year after Adolf Hitler became its leader. In 1931 he briefly ran the Baden branch of the Hitler Youth and in 1940 he joined the SS at the rank of Obersturmbannführer. Long story short; the engine of the Mazda RX-8 was based on a design by a Nazi.

*

Claudio Zampolli wasn't just responsible for the Cizeta V16T, he can also take credit for Sammy Hagar joining Van Halen. In the eighties Zampolli ran a Southern California-based business servicing supercars and had Hagar's Ferrari BB 512i in his workshop when Eddie Van Halen came by and asked who owned this car. Zampolli, knowing Van Halen had just lost lead singer David Lee Roth, told him it belonged to Sammy Hagar. "You should call him and put him in the band," the Italian added. Which is exactly what Van Halen did.

*

F1 teams don't like their drivers putting themselves at risk in the off-season which is why, in 2007, Kimi Raikkonen secretly entered (and won) a snowmobile race in his native Finland using the pseudonym 'James Hunt'.

*

The 1974 FASA-Renault 7, a saloon version of the Renault 5 developed and built in Spain, used the same glass for its windscreen and back window.

*

When Chris Bangle left his position as BMW's head of design he requested that his parting gift was an enormous block of marble from which he could make sculptures.

When the Lotus Evora went on sale in 2009 power folding mirrors were a £300 option. However, buyers soon discovered that if you prised out the mirror adjuster control, a generic Ford switch, and replaced it with the power folding compatible version of the same part, this magically activated the power folding function that had been there all along.

*

Yuri Gagarin, the first man in space, had a Matra Djet, the first mid-engined production car. The cosmonaut was presented with the sports car by the French government after an official visit to Matra, who also made aerospace equipment. It's said that Gagarin was a modest man and didn't drive his gift car very often as he found it attracted too much attention.

*

When Rover pensioned off the man who handled all their government and civil service contracts he quickly got bored and contacted an old colleague who now worked for Hyundai, offering to get them some state-funded fleet deals. Sceptical bosses at Hyundai UK said they couldn't afford to pay the man a salary but they would give him a generous commission on any deal that he landed. The chap promptly went out and sold the Metropolitan Police a huge fleet of i30s and the ball was rolling from there. This gentleman became the highest paid person on Hyundai UK's books, out-earning even the MD entirely on a commission-only deal.

*

From 1993 until 1998 the FSO Polonez was available with the 1.4-litre Rover K-series engine, although not in the UK where Rover forbad this version to be sold as one of the terms of the engine supply deal.

**THREE FACTS ABOUT SIR GRAHAM DAY
(ROVER GROUP CEO 1986-1991)**

1. He had a beard because he said not shaving gave him 10 minutes of extra reading time before work every morning.
2. He believes he was the last Canadian to receive a knighthood, gaining his title just before Britain complied with the 1988 request from Canadian Prime Minister Brian Mulroney that the British government did not confer any more titles upon his countryfolk.
3. His actual first name is Judson.

CARS WITH TRANSVERSE V8 ENGINES
Buick LaCrosse Super
Cadillac Allante
Cadillac STS
Ford Taurus SHO
Hyundai Equus
Lancia Thema 8:32
Lincoln Continental
Mitsubishi Proudia/Dignity
Oldsmobile Aurora
Volvo S80 V8
Volvo XC90 V8

The original Land Rover Discovery used visible bits from several other vehicles including doors and windscreen from the Range Rover, headlights from the Freight Rover Sherpa, and tail lights from the Austin Maestro van, the chamfered edges of which dictated the shape of the D-pillar.

*

The boot light of the MG6 had the 1980s Austin Rover logo stamped on it. It was a generic part originally used in the Austin Montego and others.

*

The phrase "simplicate and add lightness" is often attributed to Colin Chapman but had already been used by American inventor William Bushnell Stout (1880-1956) who in turn seems to have pinched it from one of his designers, Gordon Hooton.

*

Charles Leclerc's mother cuts David Coulthard's hair. Mrs Leclerc is a hairdresser in Monaco where Coulthard lives so this isn't as weird as it might sound.

*

The programme to update the classic Range Rover and Land Rover Discovery with a new, shared dashboard initially included the Defender as well. The scheme was abandoned when it was realised that it would have been too expensive to re-engineer the Defender to include the new dashboard's airbags.

*

There's an easy way to tell whether a mid-eighties Nissan Bluebird is British-made or an earlier car imported from Japan while the UK plant was getting up to speed: The glass in UK cars has Pilkington branding.

The latches used to fasten down the front and rear clamshells on the Lancia Stratos were also used to secure the lift-out roof on the Fiat X1/9.

*

The distinctive headlight mechanism of the Jaguar XJ220, in which a front-hinged flap drops down to reveal fixed lamps behind, was taken from the XJ41 'F-type' project which was cancelled in 1990. The XJ220's rear lights were from the 1989 Rover 200.

*

The middle part of the Subaru B9 Tribeca's name derived from B for 'boxer engine' and 9 from Subaru's internal classification system for different types and sizes of car.

*

When developing the W212-shape E-class, Mercedes durability engineers fitted its rear door hinges and back seats to then-current E-class taxis, reckoning that a year of cab work equated to 20 years of normal usage.

*

The European Ford Escort mk3 of 1980 and the North American Escort mk1 launched the following year looked quite similar and were meant to share multiple parts to save costs. In fact, the only component they had in common was a single bolt.

*

The machined aluminium boot hinges on the Volkswagen Phaeton were made by Campagnolo, the high-end bicycle component manufacturer.

*

The factory in Corby where they made the generic Lucas sealed beam headlight featured on British cars throughout the sixties and into the seventies was later used to manufacture Weetabix.

The 2004 facelift of the Rover 75 was done on a very tight budget with no spare cash for expensive things like re-tooling all of the lights. That's why the front indicators on the facelifted car are the ones from the original turned through 90 degrees.

*

Between 2001 and 2002 then-Nissan boss Carlos Ghosn was the star of a manga comic strip entitled The True Life of Carlos Ghosn, published in the magazine Big Comic Superior and depicting his work in turning around Nissan. Sadly the series stopped before its hero escaped to Lebanon in a cello case.

*

The 1977 Mazda 323 was sold in North America as the Mazda GLC which stood for 'Great Little Car'.

*

The Renault 21 saloon of 1986 was launched with two different wheelbases because smaller-engined models had a transverse powertrain and more powerful cars a longitudinal one. You could tell a 21's engine orientation by the gap between the edge of the front door and the wheelarch which was shorter on the lengthways-engined cars as they carried their motor ahead of the front wheels. Renault built the 21 this way because it was cheaper than developing a brand-new transverse gearbox strong enough for the larger engines. When the estate version was launched with a stretched chassis it meant the 21 range was available with four different wheelbases.

*

When the Rover 800 was launched in 1986 top models came with an all-new Honda-developed 2.5-litre V6 that weighed more than the ex-Buick 3.5-litre V8 in the 800's predecessor.

THANKING YOUS

Tom Barnard, Alan Bradley, Wayne Burgess, Chris Chapman, Craig Cheetham, Jeremy Clarkson, Mike Duff, Alex Fisk, Angus Fitton, Alex Goy, A.P. Haas, Rob Halloway, David Ingram, Nir Kahn, David Pook, Simon Rockman and Jonny Smith.

Special thanks to the wise and wonderful Keith WR Jones.

ABOUT THE AUTHOR

Richard Porter is the founder of sniffpetrol.com and the former script editor of Top Gear and The Grand Tour. He is also a columnist for evo magazine, a contributor to The Road Rat and The Sunday Times, and the writer of low-quality jokes for various TV shows. He is part of the original team of the Gareth Jones on Speed podcast and one half of Smith and Sniff, the UK's number one automotive podcast (sometimes). This is his 25th book, and his second instalment of boring car trivia. You probably knew that, on account of it being called 'Volume 2'. Duh.